Marriage
Better With Time

DR. SHIRLEY DURHAM

outskirtspress

DENVER, COLORADO

Marriage: Better With Time
All Rights Reserved.
Copyright © 2013 Dr. Shirley Durham
v1.0

Outskirts Press, Inc.
http://www.outskirtspress.com

ISBN: 978-1-4787-1221-3

Outskirts Press and the "OP" logo are trademarks belonging to Outskirts Press, Inc.

PRINTED IN THE UNITED STATES OF AMERICA

To those who are looking forward to a better marriage.

Table of Contents

Preface

Every married couple desires to have a better marriage. And the most informative place is in the word of God. And in the testimonies of those who have endured the testing of time in marriage. As you read this book, listen to wisdom and follow advice and you shall be wise.

Acknowledgments

My friends and family, who know that I like words. Words are powerful, and words are only words until you believe them.

My sons and daughters, naturally and spiritually.

To my dearest friend Rose and her husband, Dean, who befriended my husband and me by showing their love and prayers.

My beloved husband who has shown love, wisdom, and patience.

Finally I wish to thank my church family and my clients for sharing their innermost feelings. Their life experiences are helping others to overcome obstacles in everyday life.

Marriage:Better With Time

God Makes All Things Beautiful in Time
(Ecclesiastes 3:11)

Getting To Know You

Oftentimes people enter into a marriage, trying to get to know the other person; it is important that you know some things about yourself before entering into marriage. This would help avoid some pitfalls in your marriage. What are your likes and dislikes? What motivates you to do what you do? Why are you involved in the things you are associated with? What is your favorite food? Who gave you the name on your birth certificate? What does your name mean?

Never assume that your spouse knows who you are and the things you like to do. Communication is one of the important factors in a marriage. Many times you have to go back and do some reflecting, thinking on your family history. The history of your family can help you know some information about yourself.

What is your purpose for wanting to be married? People marry today for many reasons. Sometimes women attend college to get a Mrs. instead of a BS. Here are some questions that you can ask yourself before entering into marriage:

What do you enjoy doing with your spare time?

Are you a person who likes to be alone?

What are you looking for in a marriage relationship?

Do you like to eat out, or do you like home-cooked meals?

Do you understand that marriage is a lifetime commitment?

Do you want a fun relationship in marriage?

Are you a popular person, or would you like to be a popular person?

What is the most difficult experience you have had in your life?

And what did you learn from this experience?

Who was an influential person in your life?

What is your least favorite thing you like about yourself?

What is the first thing you notice about people?

What is your favorite color?

Do you like sports?

What color are your eyes?

What is the color of your hair?

Do you like to be hugged? Do you like to give hugs?

Do you like to kiss?

Do you like to read?

Do you like to spend long hours on the computer?

Do you like to travel?

Do you like to spend holidays at home?

Do you like socializing with other people?

Are you concerned about what others think about you?

Do you like what you see when you look in the mirror?

If you could change something about yourself, what would it be?

Do you have a good relationship with your parents?

Do you like to shop?

Do you seek wise counseling before making a major decision?

Do you know what the Bible says about you? It is saying that you are fearful and wonderfully made. You are made in the likeness and image of God. No greater love than this that a man would lay down his life for a friend. You are never alone. Jesus said, behold I am with you until the end of the world.

Enjoy your life with Christ; as you understand the relationship with Christ, you will understand the relationship in marriage. Marriage is until death parts us. Have you ever met someone who has a great love life and a successful career and wondered how in the world they got to be so successful? Juggling a relationship and day-to-day duties can be tricky. In a marriage you want it all, but having it all is not being realistic. You do what it takes to make the job a success. Marriage is work; it takes commitment to stay with the marriage. In marriage you face many challenges, such as sickness, debt, job loss, the loss of love ones, getting older, and other issues beyond your control.

The test of your marriage is being able to endure the unforeseen everyday life experiences. Nothing remains the same in life. The babies come and they grow up and move out. Companies downsize or close down, and your economic status changes. You have to relocate to a place you are not accustomed to. It is easy to have a bubble bath together and take a stroll on the beach, but to stay in a marriage while things are chaotic is difficult without God.

Being married has great benefits. Researches on marriage shows that people in successful marriages not only make more money but they also are healthier, live longer, and get more promotions than singles do. Fall in love with the new you. Once you get married, a change will take place and better things will lie ahead. Two is better than one; when you are down, your spouse can lift you up.

UNITING

In this world there is a lonely soul waiting to unite with another lonely soul. Each choosing through the lonely hours and meeting strangely at the most unexpected time. They begin to blend like the sun and sky into beautiful lifelong years. We are shaped and fashioned by whom we are united to.

Real love is eternal, infinite, and itself. Even when the white hair begins to show, love is always young in the heart. Uniting with the right person is like dew that falls on a rose. Uniting in true love never runs smoothly. Set me as a seal upon thine heart, as a seal upon thine arm: for love is strong as death…Many waters cannot quench love, neither can the floods drown it. ((Song of Solomon 8:6--7))

When uniting together, love and dreams must go hand in hand. In dreams and in love, there are no impossibilities. Thou shalt love the Lord thy God with all thy heart and all thy soul, and with all thy strength, and with thy entire mind; and thy neighbor as thyself. ((Luke 10:27)) Uniting in marriage is a new life.

We learn our first love through our mother's first kiss. When a child is born into this world, it is bound in love by the kind of love that explodes with tears of adoration and amazement from others. The love is so fascinating, so intense, and so pure that we cry out of joy. Love can cause our bodies to become weak and yet strong enough to enjoy life with another person.

There are some very interesting ways in which a male and fe-male come together; it is amazing how two people meet each other. Just like God created Eve from Adam's rib. Who would have thought of a woman coming from a man's rib?

Two people can meet in the strangest places. My husband, Harold, and I were serving in the same church. When I moved to another city with my job, my husband expressed to our pastor that he was interested in me. It amazes me how my son Erva was born in Germany and met his wife, Karen, who is from Denmark, at Sam Houston State University; both were born in Europe. In every courtship—I am aware that is not a twenty--first--century word, how about in every dating arrangement—everyone is on their best behavior. The ladies want to make sure everything is immaculate. The men want to look their best and make sure their car is clean and smelling good.

Uniting with your spouse has a love effect on you, not only for what you are but also what you are when you are with your spouse. When you are dating, you are on display. I must admit that when my husband asked me to marry him, I was concerned about helping him raise his three children. My husband said he had confidence in God that I was equipped to help him with his children. God created Adam, and Adam looked to the animals to see if anything was suitable for him. We can all agree that Adam made the right choice. When he saw Eve, he said wo--man. He didn't need to look to anything or anyone else. Coming together is being formed into a whole. Man without woman is incomplete. It is not good for a man to be alone. Anytime God says it is not good, be very sure it is not good.

It is a privilege to be united as husband and wife in a world where society is bringing everything together. History tells us that if a person was interested in someone, he or she would give the other person a gift. If the person was interested, he or she would receive the gift. Valentine's Day played a major part in the lives of those who wanted to express their love for someone.

In the Bible we focus on the scripture that we should not be unequally yoked. Being unequally yoked can consist of many things, including salvation, education, religion, language, geographical location, economic status, etc.

Love is the essential key to any relationship. Time is too precious to spend days, months, and years together, and then, after saying "I do" and "I will," wake up one morning and decide the two of you are not compatible. Do your homework before you say "I do" and "I will." When finding the true love of your life, ask the experts. Talk with those who have a healthy relationship. It is not advisable to enter a marriage without getting wise counseling. When a man and woman find each other, it's like finding a star that is so far out of reach and one day holding it in your hand, and not focusing on all the other stars above.

KNOWING WHAT LOVE IS

If you could take a survey on what the description of love is for different people, you would be fascinated by what others say love is. Some people may remember the song, "I Want to Know What Love Is." Love is not just based on physical attraction. Love is an emotion of strong affection and personal attachment.

People fall in love with a person without ever knowing the person's name. Have you ever looked at a couple and wondered how in the world she ended up with him or he ended up with her? One of them doesn't look so appealing to the natural eye. When I say to my husband, "I love you," I am saying I appreciate you for who you are. I celebrate the uniqueness in you; I know there is no other like you. When God made him, he broke the mold. There can be no other man like him. I truly mean that life together with him has taught me that he can bring out the best in me. I often tell him when God made him, he had me in mind. If we only think of love as a feeling, we are in for a rude awakening. Feeling can go in many different ways.

God provides us with a definition of love in 1 Corinthians 13. As you read through these verses, note that godly love is not just a warm feeling for someone:

Love is patient, love is kind. It does not envy, it does not boast, it is not proud. It is not rude, it is not self--seeking, it is not easily angered, it keeps no record of wrongs. Love does not delight in evil but rejoices with the truth. It always protects, always trusts, always hopes, and always perseveres. Love never fails. ((1 Corinthians 13:4--8a))

This puts a whole new perspective on the meaning of the words "I love you"!! Consider for a moment what this type of love looks like. "Sweetheart, I love you. What I mean is I am patient and kind with you. I do not envy you; I do not boast in front of you. I am not proud before you. I am not rude to you. I seek your good and not my own, I am not easily angered by you, and I keep no record of your wrongs. I won't hurt you." Wow!! If only we could love like that all the time.

Friendship begins with love. I believe in love at first sight. So I value the friendship that I have with my husband. We started talking long hours and days on the phone before having a dinner date. I loved him as a friend before loving him as a husband. You will know that it's real love when you can't fall asleep because your dream is now a reality. After uniting in marriage, I valued having a friend more than have the blazing romance. We celebrated birthdays, played with the children in the park, attended their sporting events, and went to open house, PTA meetings, and our children activities at school.

Taking time out for each other is therapy for your marriage. Some people think it takes money to do things together. Taking a morning or evening stroll in the neighborhood can be just as exciting as sitting down in the finest of restaurants. Make the best out of what you can afford to do, and be enthusiastic about the time you are spending together. Couples spend hundreds of dollars on trips and things. The most enjoyment is spending time together. As I listen to couples, they put more emphasis on what they saw and where they spent their vacation than on how much they enjoyed being with each other. In this fast--paced, chaotic world, it is almost impossible for a married couple to find time to spend together. Spending time with each other helps couple to express their minds and their creativity in loving, laughing, dancing, and sharing. Any couple knows it can be frustrating when you don't spend time with your spouse.

Spending time with each other is enjoyment for a couple, and it all started in the garden of Eden. A merry heart does good like a medicine but a broken spirit dries up the bone. ((Proverbs 17:22)) In the book of Galatians, it tells us to have the fruits of the spirit: love, joy, peace, patience, goodness, faithfulness, kindness, gentleness, and self--control. With these fruits of the spirit, our marriage will get better with time.

If you want to have a better marriage, consider this: your spouse comes before your father, mother, son, or daughter. Talking affection only is wasted affection. Showing affection can say what unspoken words have never said. Your spouse is with you until death. Your body belongs to your spouse. Stay away from excessive food, tobacco, drugs, or alcohol, so you may live and prosper and be in good health. The most precious gift you can give to your family is your time. Allowing your business, your hobbies, your recreation, or your job to take up all your time can destroy your family. Clean up after yourself; avoid treating your spouse like a maid. Share what you have with your spouse.

Make your spouse feel welcome to what belongs to you. Remember to tell your spouse often that you love him or her. Being faithful to your spouse is honoring your spouse. Keep your home in good condition; it is where you will both grow old together. Forgive quickly; it keeps the enemy from starting a war. Give God the glory, and your children will honor you. Have a plan of action for your family. If you fail to plan, you will plan to fail. Love is not keeping up with how much I do; but love keeps doing. You will never know what God has in store until you have weathered the storm. Love is worth fighting for. Greater love hath no man than this that a man lay down his life for his friends. ((John 15:13)) For God so loved the world that he gave his only begotten son that whosoever believe in him shall not perish but have everlasting life. ((John: 3:16))

Love is needed the most when we don't know how to love. Let us not love in word neither in tongue but in deed and in truth. ((1 John 1:18)) Aristotle said love is composed of a single soul inhabiting two bodies. Today I have a better understanding what love must be.

When Harold and I started out in our beginning stages of marriage, I thought it was all about me. I now have a better understanding that it is about us. When we are parted for any length of time, I feel like a book that is incomplete. Laughter is a way to true love. There is a place within each of us from which laughter comes out. I think it must be somewhere close to our hearts. The feelings that lead us to laugh are surely connected to what leads us to love. Love and laughter go together like prayer and devotion and like music and dance. Laughter is the manifestation of love. Love is from God.

Beloved, let us love one another: for love is of God; and every one that loves is born of God, and knows God. Beloved, if God so loved us, we ought also to love one another. No man hath seen God at any time. If we love one another, God dwells in us, and his love is perfected in us. ((1 John 4: 7, 11--12)). The Lord hath appeared of old unto me, saying, Yea, I have loved thee with and everlasting love: therefore with loving kindness have I drawn thee. ((Jeremiah 31:3)) Love is not what you are expecting to get but what you are expecting to give.

"Love is a smoke made with the fume of sighs; being purged, a fire sparkling in lovers' eyes; being vexed, a sea nourished with lovers' tears. What is it else? A madness most discreet, a choking gall and a preserving sweet." ((William Shakespeare))

There is no fear in love. But perfect love casts out fear, because fear is torment. He that fears is not made perfect in love. We love him because he first loved us. ((John 4:18--19))

"Love is not written on paper, for paper can be erased. Nor is it etched on stone, for stone can be broken. But it is inscribed on a heart, and there it shall remain forever." ((Anonymous))

My beloved spoke, and said unto me, Rise up, my love, my fair one, and come away. For, lo, the winter is past, the rain is over and gone; the flowers appear on the earth; the time of the singing of birds is come, and the turtle is heard in our land. The fig tree put forth her green figs, and the vines with the tender grapes give a good smell. Arise, my love, my fair one, and come away. O my dove, that art in the clefts of the rock, in the secret places of the stairs, let me see thy countenance, let me hear thy voice; for sweet is thy voice, and thy countenance is comely...My beloved is mine, and I am his. ((Song of Solomon 2:10--14, 16))

SHARING

While living in North Dallas, Texas before marrying Harold, I was very content with my geographical location. He lived in Fort Worth. So I wanted to keep my condo and travel back and forth. We came to an agreement that while we were looking to buy a house, we would live in Fort Worth. My husband wasn't too pleased with Dallas, and I equally wasn't too thrilled about Fort Worth.

When you decide you want to marry, it is no longer just I, it's us. We came to an agreement to live in Arlington, Texas. There is power in agreement. In marriage you have to share your re-sources and space. What belongs to you belongs to your spouse. When you love your spouse, you give him or her what he or she really needs. Your spouse needs you to be there when the money is funny and the change is strange. Your spouse needs you when the bills are due and your health is failing too.

My husband and I have been there for each other through the good, bad, and ugly. They said we wouldn't make it, and they said we wouldn't be together today. We have a testimony that if it had not been for the Lord, who was on our side, we would not be together today. Always remember to enjoy your honey-moon. Job said a man that is born of woman is but a few days full of trouble. Someone said to me, your marriage will last a year, because trouble is about to hit your marriage. I replied, "You are a little late." When I said "I do" to Harold, who was raising three children, I said the trouble was there when I said "I do" and "I will." I was reminded often that weeping may endure for a night, but joy comes in the morning. I was reminded by my grandmother to take the Lord along with you everywhere you go, because you are going to need him.

Just because you get married doesn't mean you want to have trouble. If you don't know how to pray, when you get married, you will learn shortly after the wedding to say, "I need thee, not in another second or another minute, but I need thee right now." Marriage will cause you to forget about calling someone on the phone, and it will lead you to the throne.

Some people think that marriage can survive on love alone. Please put your thinking gear on. Love can disappear or be transparent. I'm sure you've heard the phrase "I love you, but I'm not in love with you." Marriage changes the whole character when love is absent. Then you have two people taking a walk but have no clue where they are going. For example, you have a married couple who just live together. There is little to no communication. They are not involved with each other. There is no passion, caring, or concern. They are just married on paper. They are married but regretting for years that they said "I do" to each other.

After many couples have been married for about twenty--five years, they start saying, "I care about my spouse, but I have no love for him ((or her))." They express caring as if caring has pre-eminence over love. Can you care for a person without loving him or her? Or can you love your spouse without caring for him or her?

Married people care because they are married to their spouse. When you care for your spouse, it helps develop a positive out-look for your marriage.

Whatever your spouse is involved with, be his or her number one supporter. Make sure when others are cheering him on that you are right there with them. Don't just sit around looking like you have been drinking tomato juice and sucking on green persimmons. Sharing is giving up something that can benefit someone else.

Always choose your words wisely before you criticize your spouse. Ask yourself, "Is this something I would like for someone to say to me?" It's amazing that we can always dish it out, but it's hard when the shoe is on the other foot.

We learned in Sunday school do unto others as you would have them do unto you.

One of the problems that our society is facing today is a lack of honesty and commitment. Married couples will go to outside sources to get help before letting their spouse know they are having a struggle in their life. I have known people who separate from their spouses because they are afraid to tell them they have been diagnosed with a disease. I believe there should be no secrets kept from your spouse. I believe if you are covering up or hiding something, it's like Adam and Eve; you should come out of hiding.

CARING

Things can be going so well, and to your surprise, one incident can change your whole life. In 2005, I was admitted to the hospital for emergency surgery, to repair an abdominal hernia. I had joined a fitness program with a personal trainer. My first day with the personal trainer, I did one hundred sit--ups, ran twenty--five laps, did thirty minutes on a treadmill, and walked fifty laps. The next day I was not able to hold any food or liquids.

During this time of trouble, my husband was a great caregiver. He made sure I had everything I needed and wanted. You don't know how much a person really cares until you are in a helpless situation. It is not easy caring for a sick person. So if you are experiencing some issues in your life and have someone who is willing to stay by your side and help you, every opportunity you get, you should give thanks to God and give thanks to them for being there and caring for you.

The real test of your marriage is when you are going through the difficulties of life. Every unfortunate experience implies both good and bad, which is beyond your control, it will seem as though you had a dream that became a nightmare. The serenity prayer is vital in those moments, as you ask the Lord to help you to accept the things you cannot change, the courage to change the things you can, and the wisdom to know the difference.

I believe our society would be better if those who are in political position would put more concern into building healthy marriages, we would have better families and a better society. What is our society doing to help our married couples? Are we encouraging couples to stay together for the better of our society? If a marriage is under stress, what is that doing to our society? Are we making it easy for married couples to get a divorce? Marriage counseling should be available to anyone.

If you care about your spouse, there is always room for improvement. Ask your spouse for honest feedback about the things you need to work on. Be willing to be an active listener and make the adjustment as needed.

Therapon Institute's motto is people do what they do because they believe what they believe. If you care about your spouse, you will be willing to do what it takes to have a better marriage.

I believe that if marriages were better, our society would be better. If the fire is warm at home, there is no need to get wood from another forest. In other words, you have to keep the honey on the moon. Some people loose the honey while on the honeymoon. As you continue to pray and work together and each spouse gives 100 percent, your marriage will get better with time.

NURTURING

Even marriages that are very solid need nurturing. Every marriage needs some maintaining to keep it healthy. Show your spouse how much you care about maintaining your marriage. Keep the house clean. Make sure the lawn looks great. This doesn't mean you have to do it, but make sure it's done.

Share the enthusiasm when your spouse has taken the time to do something special for you. Send your wife flowers without it being a special occasion. Surprise your husband by providing his favorite meal. Go shopping with your wife and compliment the outfit that you like. Wives plan ahead. Avoid waiting until the last minute to decide to do something together.

Avoid becoming your spouse's enemy—for example, by always making everything confrontational. Be a good listener. Show your spouse you are interested in what he or she is talking about. If you're going to have intense fellowship, play the game fair. Stick with the issue you are discussing. Forget what happened in the past. Avoid belittling your spouse, and be aware that your spouse has feelings.

Don't think that just because you have an argument the marriage is over. Nothing can kill a marriage faster than being unfaithful to your spouse. Show your affection for each other. Hold your spouse's hand in public. Let your spouse know you want a hug. Your spouse doesn't always know what you need. Let your spouse know what you need. Be clear about what you want.

Your spouse needs boundaries. There will be times when your spouse needs a whole lot of "Leave me alone" time. Be understanding. Be assertive. Be compassionate. Be forgiving.

Assure your spouse you can be trusted by keeping things you've shared together in confidence. Be willing to compromise. There are certain things that you have to let go of after getting married. Use straight talk; avoid yelling and screaming to get your point across to your spouse.

There's no doubt that all couples have their problems, their moments of frustration. The success of any given marriage depends on how each spouse handles the situation. Every marriage is different. Avoid looking at someone else's marriage and comparing your marriage to theirs.

When my husband and I were into a year of our marriage, I was sharing with someone how I didn't understand the ups and down in marriage. This couple had been married for over ten years. I was doing all the sharing, and they would say, "Just pray!!" When Harold and I would have an outing with them, it seemed as though they had the perfect marriage. Then I received a phone call from them saying that they were getting a divorce. My husband and I went to their house, and boxes were everywhere; I was discombobulated. It taught me that everything that looks good is not what it seems. Harold and I prayed with them. They are still married and going on thirty years.

Fall in love with your spouse over and over again. Make every effort to be so in love. Falling in love is not hard; that's why it's called falling in love. It happens so fast. My husband sent me a teddy bear in the mail before we were married. I had not shared with him that I liked teddy bears. I was so surprised. I was smiling so big; it was like the smile could not go away.

After a few years of marriage, the euphoria of love seems to diminish. It is a natural stage for all marriages. You wake up one day and wonder, "Did I marry the wrong person?" With some nurturing in your marriage, you will understand it gets better with time.

PLANNING

Marriage brings a change in the newlyweds' financial situation that will affect all parts of their life together—everything from financial goals to credit card debt will bring new challenges to the marriage. Understanding how to move through the changes can be challenging, but planning ahead will allow you to build a strong financial foundation for you and your spouse.

One of the many obstacles to overcome is dealing with separate bank accounts. Should you keep separate accounts, or should you have a combination of joint and separate accounts? Whatever you decide, this is an important first step to talk about when getting married.

It is generally a good idea to consider a combination of both joint and individual accounts. The joint account should be used for family expenses: the mortgage or rent, utilities, bills, groceries, and so on. In addition, each person should have an individual account for personal spending, or fun money. This can help simplify things when it comes to bills yet also helps keep personal spending in check.

Married couples should have a budget. Not only is it important to decide how to keep track of your money in the bank, but this is the time to get serious about creating a family budget. Your new spouse will contribute new financial issues such as debt, assets, bills, and even savings to your household. Even if you had created a budget for yourself in the past, these new pieces of financial challenges will undoubtedly change the new budget.

Take some time to sit down with your spouse and look at your combined cash flow. What debt payments will you both have? How much can you save? Can you find ways to combine expenses, such as switching to the same wireless phone plan? Answering these questions together will help you develop the most realistic budget for your married life.

Planning for the unexpected can be beneficial for your marriage. Now that you're married, you will also need to make important decisions about insurance and estate planning. If both of you work and are covered by a health plan through an employer, it is important to take a look at which plan will be the most beneficial. Getting married is one of the life events that allow you to change your health insurance election without waiting for the open enrollment period, so use this time wisely.

In addition to health insurance, this is a good time to discuss life insurance. When you are single and without children, there is little need for life insurance since nobody is depending on your income but you. When you get married, you should discuss what would happen if your spouse was left to support your household alone. Having life insurance would not be devastating unless you couldn't afford to pay the premium.

Every working couple should have a retirement plan. Once you have your benefits squared away, you'll also want to take a look at beneficiaries on retirement plans, pensions, and IRAs and ensure that your assets are disbursed properly when you die.

Finally, it all comes down to communication. Many married couples find it hard to talk about money, and this can lead to problems in the future. You may think in retrospect about the stress that money can cause when you're single, so imagine how stressful it can be when you are married. Make it a responsibility for you and your spouse to come together often to discuss the assets and debts that you have acquired, so neither spouse is left in the dark about the finances. If the finances are funny, the romance will be as well.

FOREVER FOR LIFE

There was a song that went something like this: Always and forever each moment with you, is just like a dream to me that somehow came true. It is through Jesus Christ that you can have a forever life with your spouse. Jesus said in Matthew 10:10, I am come that you might have life and that you may have it more abundantly.

Some couples will say if you make it through the first five years, the rest is a smooth road. Every year is a stepping stone. You can start out with everything going smoothly, but just like the signs on the side of the highway that say "rough road ahead," you will experience rough roads quite often.

You take every anniversary as success. One phone call can change your life. For example, you have relatives who want to come and stay with you. Parents get sick and you choose to take care of them. Nieces and nephews want to spend the summer at your house. Grown children move back home or need help financially. Your spouse gets sick or you get sick. You have a car accident. You have to relocate with your job. The doctor just gave you bad news. The list can go on.

As a married couple, if you survive for any length of time, you can advise others with encouragement on what to do and what not to do. Robert Frost said that marriage begins in delight and ends up in wisdom. It takes effort by both spouses to work toward a better marriage. Some people are content with a chaotic marriage. They are OK with things being out of balance; that is the lifestyle they are accustomed to. They saw the way their parents and their grandparents lived in marriage, so this is their learned behavior.

It is possible to continue a passionate, romantic love life with your spouse long after the honeymoon. The Bible is the greatest book ever written that teaches a married couple how to have a life forever. The Song of Solomon, a love letter, can help a married couple keep the honey on the moon long after the honeymoon is over. Keeping the wood on the fire will keep the fire burning in your marriage for a lifetime.

Concentrate on developing an intimate marriage. Nurture your spouse emotionally. Touching is showing love; surprise your spouse by walking behind him or her. Stroke some part of his or her body, showing you care without saying a word.

Leave the negatives out that could change the way your spouse sees you. Live in an environment with a positive outlook on the future. Be quick to forgive and move forward. Look at it this way: the automobile has a large windshield, and the rearview mirror is small. There are better things in front of you than what is behind you. So keep moving forward.

Avoid sharing your problems about your marriage with the opposite sex. Feelings can be very tricky. The other person begins to feel sympathetic about what you are sharing, and you become emotionally involved with that person; you start thinking you are in love. Wrong!! You just got tricked. Emotions will be aroused if you think that someone cares about you because that person gives you a little attention and his or her time. When things are going downhill in your marriage, spend some time with each other and show some concern toward each other.

The message of feelings is true to anyone who has been in love. It plays a vital part in marriage. A marriage cannot survive on just one person having feelings. The love must be the same

Love and feeling is like walking on air, moving ahead together on solid ground. And delight is transformed by wisdom into something even better: a life together.

FEELINGS

No person who gets married is not looking to be with his or her spouse forever, unless the person is not in his or her right mind. Being in love usually leads to both spouses having the same desire to make a new life together. Having a commitment and exemplifying the love you have for each other can lead to a better marriage.

Feelings are the music of life and the magic that makes marriage exciting, pleasurable, and satisfying. Let's touch on the magic by analyzing what happens when a man and a woman fall in love. It is important to understand the dynamics of falling in love because they are the very dynamics you will want to keep alive in your marriage relationship. Don't take them for granted because the weight of everyday living can smother the magic of love before you realize it.

Two people falling in love is a powerful emotional event. That it happens to both lovers at the same time intensifies the sense of delight. There is the thrill of newness and a sense of wonder as if the two lovers have entered into a new reality. This is almost like time traveling in space.

The term "falling" accurately depicts the suddenness and drama of the situation. The phrase "in love" correctly implies that the lovers are no longer where they were. They have left themselves as individuals to dwell in a new place together.

When love is genuine, the lovers long to be together. In fact they may even feel shock waves of emotion when they must be apart, incomplete when they are separated. This powerful sense of need for the other may express itself in a sensation of homesickness. This happens when they are bonded emotionally and now crave that feeling of security. For where your treasure is there will your heart be also. ((Matthew 6:21)) Feelings are so fragile and explosive that they must be handled with special care. How you consider your partner's feelings will tell a great deal about you as a lover. And we have already suggested that the feelings of love are the treasure within the earthen vessel of marriage, but they can change unexpectedly, so never look to them as the last word. Always remember, you are more than feelings.

Throughout the Bible, God reveals a whole tapestry of feelings. The Song of Solomon offers a vivid display of the feelings of love experienced by a bride and her husband. But nowhere in the New Testament does God ever command us to feel anything. Rather, he would have us behave in certain ways or adopt a certain attitude, which will produce certain feelings. It is a principle worth learning: if we obey God with right actions, the right feelings will soon follow.

VACATIONS

Give your marriage the best; take vacations. If you only dream and never make your dream a reality, it is just a dream. There are many married couples who have been married for years and have never taken a vacation. In counseling we often use the phrase "If you always do what you have always done, you'll get what you always got." Choose your destination from around the world. Make your dreams come true in your marriage.

Some of the best advice we received from my mentor, Diane Winfrey, was to always save and plan for a vacation because it would be good therapy for our marriage. We took that advice and have taken a vacation every year together.

Add some spice to your life. Going to visit family is not a vacation. I believe that married couples should have a vacation with and without their children. There is nothing like having some fun, running in the sand, and watching the waves make a beautiful sound. You and your spouse can play, eat, shop, relax, and explore the beauty of God's handiwork.

These are some of the places where we have traveled outside the USA: Bahamas, Paris, London, Israel, Germany, Spain, Italy, Turkey, China, Belgium, and Hawaii. Your happiness is the greatest compliment you can give your love spouse. Our friend Corlee Kent, a friend in high places, helped make some of these trips possible.

FAITHFULNESS

Each person can have some qualities in which they can contribute to their marriage. As a spouse, how would you answer this question? What one quality do you believe will contribute most to the continuing development of love and growth in your marriage relationship?

Think about it!! Finding the most satisfactory answer to this question was recently put to a husband and wife who have loved each other for more than a quarter century. Their responses were completely different, and since each gave an answer without knowing how the other responded. Consider their answers. What essentials have been at work to make their marriage last?

Faithfulness in marriage means firmly adhering to the commitment you have made. In both attitude and action, you are loyal, true, and constant to your marriage partner. Faithfulness implies duty, with an allegiance, vows, and promises to live up to. The husband and wife who are faithful to each other will enjoy the journey of life together. First, a faithful couple must never allow a third person to intrude into their love relationship. When you are faithful to your husband or wife, who is truly faithful, you live out your loyalty to one another not out of duty, but out of joy.

When you are faithful to your spouse, you not only avoid adultery but you also don't even give the appearance of interest in another person. Your spouse should never feel the need to compete with someone else for your attention or admiration.

There is a requirement of loving your spouse in ways that meet his or her needs and deepest desires. We can never plead ignorance as to how to do this. God has shown us how to faithfully love one another: Submitting yourselves one to another in the fear of God. Wives, submit yourselves unto your own husbands, as unto the Lord. For the husband is the head of the wife, even as Christ is the head of the church, and he is the savior of the body. Therefore as the church is subject unto Christ, so let the wives be to their own husbands in everything. Husbands, love your wives, even as Christ also loved the church, and gave himself for it. ((Ephesians 5:21--25))

Faithfulness begins as a choice. It is fact, always a choice. As one Christian therapist has explained:

Central to marriage is this choosing process wherein a unique relationship with one person is established. What keeps it vital is faithfulness, which continues to choose the same person in the mist of pain, frustration, and disillusionment. Apart from this, the institution of marriage cannot sustain the blush of its initial days or the vows of its spouse.

Faithfulness in marriage means firmly adhering to the commitment you have made. In both attitude and action, you are loyal, true, and constant to your spouse.

COMMUNICATION

The link that holds a marriage together is communication. If you have good communication in your marriage, you will find it strengthening and wholesome in your marriage journey. You need the knowledge and understanding of one another for intimate closeness. Don't assume your husband or wife knows what you desire. The interchange of information and ideas helps you to work together as husband and wife on the journey through your life together. Married couple will have time of intense fellowship, which other people my call moments of frustration. The ability to work out your differences and resolve your conflicts will allow you to become mature, in life.

You must have continued touching and contact to grow together in the same direction, and to be there to support each other during the changes of difficult times of life. Couples trying to continue in a marriage without communication will encounter major problems.

When Harold and I counsel married couples, communication lines are almost always severed in their marriage. Studies of researchers in marriage have found out that 90 percent of marriage problems are due to a communication breakdown. It is easy when you are dating, lulled by soft lights and romance, to assume that you communicate well. However, during the moments of intense marriage fellowship, character defects are brought to the surface. Married couples seem as if they are not able to communicate. When couples agree they can't communicate, they want to give up on their marriage.

Researchers report that most husbands express marital dissatisfaction through anger and withdrawal, while most wives show
their dissatisfaction through depression and withdrawal. In all
marriages, the withdrawal into silence is devastating and should
be a red flag that something needs attention.

The most noticeable communication in a marriage is silence.
"Silent" and "listen" are spelled with the same letters. If the husband and wife are both silent and listening at the same time,
nothing is getting accomplished. When the husband and wife are
not communicating, all is not lost. No couple needs to get to that
point. Any communication problem can be worked out. When
Harold and I got married, we wanted to be careful not to hurt
each other's feelings so we often said, "How should I say this?"
As you learn from each other, you develop skills and practice.
You just say what needs to be said. However, be respectful to
each other.

Take some time to think about your communication skills. Do
you pause and evaluate before addressing an issue? Are you at
liberty to express your feelings at the spur of the moment with
each other? Husbands, do you hear what your wife is really saying? Wives, do you understand what your husband is really feeling? When you hit a pothole in your communication with your
spouse, keep trying. As you continue in your marriage and work
on communication, it will get better with time.

ENJOYING THE JOURNEY

On May 13, 1993, the day Harold and I said our wedding vows to each other, our pastor made sure that before we said "I do," our children had to stand with us. Harold had three children from a previous marriage, and I had one from a previous marriage. It was quite an awakening for me. I thought I had planned a trip to Paris and ended up in Australia. Most people, if they had their druthers, would choose Paris over Australia. I couldn't wait to go on our honeymoon and spend a wonderful time together. Well, it didn't happen the way we had planned. The book of Proverbs 19:21 ((NIV)) tells us that many are the plans in a person's heart, but it is the Lord's purpose that prevails. We had to make the best of the situation. Sometimes we should just enjoy where we are; however, we can become engrossed in our feelings instead of enjoying where we are at the time. Someone said when life hands you lemons, make lemonade. One thing we had was a spark in our eyes. Anytime you have a spark, you can start a fire. We wanted to be with each other; if you want to be with someone you love, there is no mountain too high and no valley too low that can keep you apart. In marriage there are many mountains and valleys. Oftentimes people find themselves discouraged when things are not going their way. It is so easy to throw in the towel and quit. I beseech you therefore, brethren, by the mercies of God, that you present your bodies a living sacrifice, holy, acceptable unto God, which is your reasonable service. And be not conformed to this world: but be transformed by the renewing of your mind, that you may prove what is that good, and acceptable, and perfect, will of God. ((Romans 12:1, 2))

So here we are in our nineteenth year of marriage. Our five children have attended college, and they are productive citizens in our society. In order to leave a legacy with your children, it should start with how they see you love one another. Our daughter Porshua, who is the last child to graduate from high school and is now attending college, wanted to know what we were going to do when it was just the two of us at home. We told her we are going to continually enjoy each other. Life is not supposed to stop because the children have moved away from home. It is now time to live, as John 10:10 states, live life in abundance. Some people make the mistake of putting all their time into their children, and when the children have moved out, they don't know what to do with themselves. If you are enjoying your spouse now, when the children move away, you will not be mystified about the change.

Harold and I were advised by a sister in the church, who encouraged us to plan a time every year to take a vacation, just the two of us. We would put money aside so we could spend time together without the five children. This time allowed us to enjoy one another, to discuss the problems we were facing, and to share our thoughts and feelings. Also we would pray for each other, that God would help us and give us wisdom to deal with our problems so we could love one another and be patient and forgiving.

We go through life focusing and having intense fellowship on things that are really not that important. Oftentimes it's attention we want from our spouse.

I'm reminded of a story about a husband and wife who were having an intense moment in their marriage. The wife took her ring off and threw it across the room. The husband began looking under the furniture and saying to his wife, "Do you know how much that ring cost?" His wife began to cry and, in an outburst, said, "I'm so sorry." The writer implied that if only the husband would have put as much effort into seeing what his wife's problem was by embracing her and saying, "I love you and I want to find out what the problem is," maybe her ring wouldn't have left her finger.

I also read about a husband and wife who were having such a busy day that the husband was attending to the baby while his wife was cleaning and doing things around the house. The wife became angry because it looked like the husband and the child were having so much fun playing on the floor and laughing together. The wife said to her husband, in a moment of disgust, "I am going to pick up a few items from the store." She left the house so upset that she put her purse in the back and left the door open. As she backed out of the garage, the open back door of the car hit the corner of the wall and bent the car door. Her husband heard this loud noise and ran to the garage to see what had happened. He looked at the car door and then looked at his wife. He reached into the car and gave her a big hug and said the door could be replaced.

It was about a year into our marriage, and the kids and I were at an oriental rug auction. Harold was at work. I was so excited to hear the bidding on a $6,000 rug start at $500. One man said $650 and another man said $850 and I said $1,000. The man said, "Sold to the lady." My son Erva looked at me and said, "Mom, oh my God, what have you done?" My son Donelle said, "My daddy is going to be so upset." I was so afraid to tell my husband I had spent that kind of money without talking it over with him. I called Harold at work to let him know I had made a mistake by paying that much money for a rug without discussing it with him. He said, "We will talk about it when I get home." The hours seemed so long as I waited for him to come home. When he got home, he gave me a hug, rolled on the rug, and said a rug costing that much surely had something good about it.

Sometimes, when your spouse has made a bad decision, you have to think about what is best for the situation at the time. The decision was not going to change: the money was spent and we could not get it back. There are many journeys in marriage. The best way to deal with them is to go through them, and as you go through them, you will come to learn how to enjoy the journey.

PRAYING TOGETHER

Prayer is just simply talking to God: Let us know that we should always pray and not faint. ((Luke 18:1)) You don't have to be afraid to come to God. We can come boldly to the throne of God. ((Hebrews 4:16)) You and your spouse are not praying to change God's mind; it helps you both to accept the will of God in your life.

It is a wonderful thing when you and your spouse can come together in prayer. When Harold and I did for the first time, I tell you, I felt like it was not normal. I thought when you came to God it should be a secret moment between you and God, and nobody should know what you are saying in your prayer time. My husband and I pray together sometimes but not often. Whenever we come together to pray, we usually are facing some challenges that are afflicting both of us, or sometimes it is to pray together for others. When we both know someone else is in need, we come together and pray.

When Harold and I do come together to pray, it brings a closer connection between us, and we feel the unity it brings when we pray together. Just as we spend mealtimes together, we pray together. Christmas morning was a wonderful time for me. I would wake everyone up, and my husband would lead us in prayer. He would start out by giving God thanks for keeping us together.

We also pray alone. It is surprising when I talk with other Christian couples who say they don't pray with their spouse. Harold and I believe in the power of prayer. My prayer time is most often three o'clock in the morning, every day no matter where I am staying. It amazes me that no matter what time I go to bed, or how late I go to bed, God will wake me up at three o'clock. I was visiting my friend Rose and her family in New Jersey, and when I woke up, the clock said four o'clock. I felt disappointed because I wanted to stick with my prayer time. However, I prayed at four o'clock. After getting up for the day, I realized I had kept my prayer time: I was still on Texas time, which was one hour behind.

A minister, who was about seventy, brought his niece and her husband to me and asked if I could give them godly counseling. After talking with them and sharing scriptures from the Bible, the uncle said, "I want both of you to kneel before God and pray. I want you to ask God for help." The wife started praying, "Lord, I ask you to help my husband…" The uncle stopped her and said, "You pray for God to help you and let your husband pray for help for himself." The uncle told his niece that before you can pray for help for someone else, you need to ask God for help for yourself.

Most of the time we want to focus on the needs of others. As the gospel song says "Lord, it's me standing in the need of prayer." During our prayer time, we find ourselves saying, "Lord, help my spouse." If we could look at ourselves and not our spouse and keep our temple clean, we would better know how to pray for our spouse.

A couple came to get marriage counseling. This was their second session. I asked the husband if he would like to close the session with prayer. He said, "Wow, I have never prayed in front of anyone." After he finished praying, he said to his wife, "Baby, maybe we should pray together." She replied, "I didn't know you could pray like that."

In October 2011, I was asked by a member of the church if I would pray for her during her wedding ceremony. I asked her, "What do you want me to pray about?" She said, "Just let God give you what to pray for." The week of her wedding I was so tense about what to pray for. So I asked God how I should pray for this person. I began to think about what a godly man would want for a wife, and I began to write out a prayer for a bride.

This is the prayer I wrote:

Lord, thank you for Crista, who wants to be a wife. Thank you for allowing her husband to find her in the midst of countless women who want to be married. Crown her with wisdom from on high. Let her create an atmosphere in their home that would welcome your presence and make her husband feel honored to have her as his wife. Let her be a woman who prays for her husband. Let her know that you have an open--door policy, that she can cast all her cares on you. Let her be a loving and caring wife. Let her be an example for other young women. Use her to bring glory to you, Lord. In the name of Jesus, Amen.

During your and your spouse's prayer time, let there be a time of silence where you can hear what God is saying to your spirit. Pray together as often as possible. Keep in mind that praying together has to be developed and it gets better with time. Try not to override what the other one is praying about. Always come humbly together. Remember that you are one, aiming for the same thing, that is, having a better marriage with time.

THINGS NOT CONFRONTED WILL NOT CHANGE

Man and woman see something in each other that they are attracted to. Without the opposite sex, it is hard to function as a whole person. A distance comes between a husband and wife when they have those intense moments of disagreement; this causes to some degree little or no communication. To identify problems, each person should express what makes him or her feel uncomfortable. For instance, if your spouse is not neat, it makes you become judgmental. Whenever you become judgmental, your spouse becomes defensive.

Conflicts can be a tough challenge when you enter into marriage.

The first year of our marriage, Harold and I were trying to make sure what we had to address was not going to be offensive to the other, so we would somewhat walk on eggshells to keep our conflicts from becoming intense fellowship. Matthew 18:7 lets us know that offenses will come. In our confronting, we should remember what Isaiah 1:18 says: come let us reason together. In order to get the problem solved, it takes the husband and wife coming together to work out the problem.

Conflicts are usually brought on by issues in which a couple disagrees with a person's action. This can sometimes lead to an argument, frustration, or even separation and divorce. If you ignore a problem, it will only get worse. The more you allow the problem to remain without being confronted, the more you are hurting your marriage and yourself. And the problem will get increasingly worse. Be fair about the situation. Give your spouse time and liberty to express his or her side. Avoid thinking that you have all the answers to the situation—for example, saying to your spouse, I know why you did that or said what you said. Trying to be the judge in your marriage will only make the problem progressively worse. The mission you want to accomplish is for your spouse and you to have a clear understanding and come to an agreement to solve the problem.

Sometimes when you are trying to solve conflicts, your voice seems to get loud. When Harold and I feel that our voices are escalating, we say to each other, "Lower your voice," to let the other know we are hearing the tone changing the situation from trying to solve the problem to starting another problem. Proverbs 15:1 tells us a soft answer turns away wrath but grievous words stir anger. When you see your communication is turning into a shouting match and nothing is being resolved, stop talking, go into another room, and say to your spouse, "We need to discuss this at a later time." Some couples have a difficult time accepting that all marriages have conflicts. Many married couples find that conflicts are great. It helps to bring out the inability to deal with the hidden problems that need to be confronted.

When dealing with conflict, the healthiest way is to deal with it straight on. However, make sure both parties are ready to address the issues. Avoid covering up when trying to fix it up. If you don't deal with the conflict straightforwardly, you will suffer the consequences later, and the problem will be worse than when it started. Conflicts can make a better marriage. It can bring you closer together and help you overcome the fear every time you have to deal with an issue. It can be constructive and helpful to both parties if they feel loved and respected.

Here are some problems in marriages that need to be confronted so the issues can be solved:

Your spouse is threatening to leave.

Your spouse thinks your marriage is falling apart.

Your marriage has fallen into a rut.

Your spouse thinks that cheating is occurring.

Your spouse feels there is too much arguing, fighting, and bickering.

Your spouse feels there is little to no affection or intimacy.

Your spouse feels taken for granted or not appreciated or wanted.

Your spouse feels the marriage is boring and you have fallen out of love.

It is advisable that you deal with each situation one at a time. When you try to deal with more than one problem at a time, you find yourself operating in an overloaded conflict. For example, when you put too many clothes in a washer at one time, the washer starts to shake and to protrude from the bottom or the top. So the problem is not resolved.

Rescue your marriage before it reaches the critical point. Dealing with the conflicts of marriage can help you and your spouse avoid problems that can occur in the future. When you don't have the answers to the problems, saying "I love you" to your spouse is not a cure--all, but it really helps.

MY SPOUSE NEEDS AS MUCH AS MY CHILDREN

My mother, Eloise Givens, and my grandmother, Vessie Jackson, were great examples of how to be a loving, caring wife and mother. They both were stay--at--home mothers who loved their families. My mother would not only show us but also say to us, "I love you." She would give us compliments and tell us how beautiful we were. When we came home from school, dinner was always cooking, and you could smell the aroma of food before you made it to the door. If my father wasn't home before it was time for dinner, my mother would not allow us to have dessert until my father had the first slice. By my mother doing this for my father, it helped me to know that she wanted to have the best for him.

My husband is the king of our castle. I hold him in high esteem. He is a man of God, who has provided for our family in rain, sleet, and snow. There was a time when I would say to him, "It's too bad the streets are icy." He would say, "I'll be OK." He would make sure the children and I "had everything" we needed, before he would consider himself.

In my observation as a pastor's wife, I would hear the ladies say, "I give honor to my pastor…he is a great and wonderful pastor… I love him so much." The years would pass and I would not hear them complimenting their husbands. When I had the opportunity to teach, I would say to the ladies, "I don't understand how you can build up the pastor and not give honor to your husband." Their husbands go to work, making sure their families have the things that they need. Come to church and serve the people of God. Don't hold another man in higher esteem than your own husband. Appreciate the husband you have and give compliments to him. I try my best to be my husband's number one cheerleader.

There are times, but not enough, that the question is asked: who comes first, my spouse or my children? Let me be the first to tell you that your children will grow up and will make their own decisions on who they are going to marry and where they want to live. And it will be you and your spouse. The word of God tells us to leave and cleave. It is better to cleave before they leave. The first priority should be your spouse. If your children are sick or helpless, of course you take that into consideration. Our daughter Porshua was concerned with what her mom and dad were going to do since she was the last child out of five leaving home and going off to college. We assured her we would really be able to live. My husband told her one thing for sure: he would receive a raise, and the water bill and electric bill would go down, so there would be an increase in the income.

Your children are with you for eighteen to twenty--two years; your spouse is with you for a lifetime. Some children may say, "I'm your child forever, and your spouse could end up leaving you." What would make them come up with that assumption? I say, by what they see from you and your spouse. If your children are first and not your spouse, you are ruining your marriage and your children. Your children will learn more by you being an example than by you saying what they should be. They will see how you put your spouse first, and your children will learn how to be a good spouse themselves.

CHANGES IN MARRIAGE

We must understand that what people did during the World War II era and now is quite different. During that time, marriage was focused on family. The wife was excited about having children. She would stay home, and the husband was the wage earner and made the large financial decisions.

Love was shown by keeping your responsibility to your duties for the family.

During the time of Vietnam, married people believed that one income was not enough to support the family, so the wife started working outside the home, and the husband began to take on some chores in the home. I can remember when my mother was home and all the children were off to school; she wanted to work outside the home. With my father's approval, she took on a job working nine to five. Our home became chaos; no one was there when we came home from school, and we were eating dinner late in the evening. That only lasted for two weeks, because my father told my mother her first responsibility was home. In this generation it seems that when people get married, children are not usually in the plan of their life. Married people should not be concerned about the change in society to be politically correct but to be biblically correct in marriage.

Every marriage has a cycle. In the first stages of your marriage, you couldn't do without your spouse. You anxiously waited for his or her call. You anticipated his or her touch and hearing the sweet words spoken about you. Falling in love with your spouse was not something difficult. As a matter of fact, it was easy. You really didn't have to do anything. This is the reason it is called falling in love. There is a saying from the older generation: "I was swept off my feet." Well I was!! I loved my husband's voice and his nice body. When we got engaged, I came to hear him preach with my brother Willard. He had sweat pouring from his face. That seemed interesting.

As you journey through married life, you will find out that you will begin to take on the attributes of your spouse. When Harold and I got married, Harold was quiet and conservative. I was the adventurous one, willing to take risks and new challenges. As years begin to pass, I became more like Harold, and he began to be outgoing and accept new challenges. When we began to experience uncertain times in the economy and people were losing their jobs, he told the church, "If opportunity doesn't knock, then you build the door." This can be applied in our marriages. If you find yourself bored with your marriage, you become inventors of how to make your marriage better. We neglect the three--letter word "ask." The acronym is Ask--Seek--Knock. Ask for help. Continue to seek until you get what you need. Knock until you get an answer. Find someone who is mature in his and her marriage and ask questions.

There is something that we can learn about change: it will never change. Changes will happen, ready or not. When you first got married, you may have been a Coke bottle, and as time passed you became a jug. You can look in the mirror and see change, sometimes more often than you would like to. Change should always be for the betterment of your life. Change is helpful in building a better marriage over time. When you have survived over a period of time, you will not be the same. All things work together for the good of those who are called according to God's purpose. ((Romans 8:28)) If God brought you to it, he can bring you through it.

ENJOYING THE BLESSINGS

The unique beauty of marriage is looking over the years of ups and downs in your relationship, and seeing that you are still together and identifying that as a blessing.

Praise God for allowing you to celebrate your years of marriage. Arrange a time to be available to be with your spouse all day without any interruption. Take a vacation. Have a candlelight dinner. Listen to music that will encourage your marriage to be stronger for the years to come. Pay homage to those who have been instrumental in your marriage.

Get beyond shoulda, coulda, and woulda, and start where you are now. It's been said many times that there is no such thing as a perfect marriage. I wholeheartedly agree. I can say that if you surround yourself with couples who have the same focus— they want a successful marriage—you will see progress.

Embrace the moments you have enjoyed being with your spouse. Pick up some fresh ideas to bring excitement to your marriage. Share with your spouse the things that make you enjoy being married to him or her.

Marriage is a covenant and not a contract. A piece of paper does matter, but it is the vow that is important to the marriage. The difference is a contract says if this marriage doesn't meet my needs, it's over. A covenant is the seal that both parties agree they are not going to give up on their marriage, no matter what comes their way. Our society seems to be more concerned or caught up in having romance as the most important part of a marriage. Some people like to say marriage is for now and not forever. Enjoy the blessings of marriage now so there will be a forever.

Being married causes couple to have a closer relationship with God and bring more joy into their lives. The question is often asked, "Is there such a thing as a happy marriage?" Yes, there is, if God is the center of the marriage. The Bible has provided all the ingredients to have a successful marriage. If you are willing to make sacrifices, to do what it takes to have a happy marriage, then you can enjoy the blessing of a marriage better with time.